Old Burn, New Burn

Spontaneous Gambol

Two Collections of Poetry

by

Russell Buker

Published by Piscataqua Press
A project of RiverRun Bookstore
142 Fleet St., Portsmouth NH 03801

www.piscataquapress.com
www.riverrunbookstore.com

ISBN: 978-1-939739-75-9
Printed in the United States of America

To my father
whose stories still resonate

Old Burn,
New Burn

Foreword

The Queen of poetry is not dead by any means and yet one wonders where the sound and fury of poetry has gone and tomorrow and tomorrow and tomorrow creeps. Could it be that our world is too crowded and macabre for many of us to utilize any common sense in interpreting our raison d'etre, one that merely follows the dictates of multi-nationals and their bottom line no matter the consequences while poetry increasingly renders mere anecdotes flipping, *show me, don't tell me,* on its back and exposing its yolk to the frying eyes of readers who remain on a rudder-less voyage that knows no anchors?

I had just delivered a commencement speech at a high school that I had taught in for a considerable time and one of the teachers asked what I was doing in my retirement. Oh, I have been writing and writing books of poetry, I replied. Why on earth would you do that, he asked, nobody reads poetry anymore. The academic system grinds out way too many poets/writers every year and they in turn grind out obligatory work to be printed in the industry off presses that have been created to accommodate them. Passionless stuff, yet passion matters in poetry and one of the many reasons poetry seemingly inspires so little passion among people in contemporary society is that it has ceased communicating with people and is much too concerned with just acceptance in its industry.

I think I forgot this arguing back and forth. Reality is flexible and depends where you are. I'm not attempting to sell and realize my audience so far is small-quite possibly another John Clare among the many MFA sophisticates- but I enjoy writing, nor do I worry about my window of opportunity as I find the value of credit is actually in the doing. I also agree with Yeats' sentiment as he looked around his club in Dublin where the poets hung out: "there are too many of us," but my being away from the mainstream for the most part, I would hesitate to be the one who says, You stay, You go. No thank you I'm off to feed my feral cats. They are the real poets knock, knocking on fortune's door.

—Russell Buker

Contents

Russell Buker

But

Finally got up the courage
to do
what I should have done
years ago

Looked both ways as
I
raced back from such
solitude

though the setback seemed
incidental
to the cat eating winter
sprouted

oat grass while first the edges
of a
sleeve, vessel, dried slowly
restricting

any soft afterglow from
monuments
built by myself over the
years

of pure excitement,
pancaking
of delusion as the four
walls

I crafted turned to heavy
doors
that would not open
from

the inside which I'm
told
is against all building
codes

There is

no gulf resembling
quite
like the half sleep
where
whales rise up to
gulp
to seem we are
emptying
our cereal bowls

And the odd shark
rides
a wave of its own
marking
his surf onto our
beach
snapping at legs and
anything
else beach resting

My recliner chained
against
the surge will not
allow
reading. How will I
know
how far removed this
pleasantly
colored bird hovering,

attempting to dial a
correct
feeding beak for here
and
then the chain snaps
loud
enough in the swoon
room:
and you were saying?

What if

you stop remembering loss with
your minds quick forgiveness
of the long, blue-tang of ice?

What's worse than this finding
of having been off the trail too,
too long: a wood thrush song

gone silent from within its secrecy
while the bark and leaves of shrubs
are beside themselves in the long

stillness of an early winter Yugen
that triggers silver, teary responses
from somewhere other than words

Adjoining

Is it
human I thought
to
repeal the order
of
my older language's
sleeping

So long
as both our dust
lies
wind protected
sun
will dry delighted
squeals

being
together this long
we
can out wait the
pelting
wisdom of rain,
make

something of our-
selves
again: fluent
bones
holding fluid tongues,
finger-
prints never seen
before

Deny

me all you
want
standing so aloft
on
aching, spasmined
shoulders

I should not
have
come out to
greet
such a westing
gaze

hovering above
tree-
line with your own
noon
time's dispersing
air

After

I borrowed neglect,
borrowed a friends
tweed jacket
with money
long forgotten in two
pockets

I fought hard
to give it back
wordless-
credit may become
mine,
nothing

I have no piece
to end this all
all those years
tossing trash
onto the shore's
salty teeth

breath of destruction
our construction
to kill, economic
comic exposition and
no escaping
raking the coals,

yesterday's fire,
renewed
to kill again
encumbers
of the Global State
staunchly

Old Burn, New Burn

protected
by our love of country,
bloody peace
with money grafted
to those convenient
friendlies

who shed no tears
or taps-
unsettling as they
are to us-
mourning nothing
looking, looking
for places, to stash
their cash

Possibly

it is our soggy nature,
distrust,
to fear each other.

I remember the two
of us
painting way through

the sun and into early
darkness
and faltering we made

it back to the kitchen
with one
candle for light as we

ate whatever was left
to us
before feeling our way

toward the morning's
sight
of how your talent had

stopped whenever elastic
paint
had brushed so close

to those dim intersections
that I
foolishly rushed through,

hastily perhaps, to land
feebly
while you peered over

your full edge imploring
come back
we'll finish later, later

Crazy

but spring is much
later
yet another spring
storm
falls on me with
damp
flakes that try and warm
them-
selves on me. My
plan
this year is trap the
last
flake, also a raccoon,
in a
quiet wire opening
smelling
disgustingly human: a
prayer
to grasp the recently re-
awakened
flakes and raccoon shivering
alive
from inside winter's guest
house
that slows all of us out-
side
ourselves, Machiavellian Cardinals,
hands
on each other's hips dream
pure
and rapid how to humanely
trap
those newly moving flakes,
raccoons,
and squeeze their humic
coil
to a slow, Adriatic summer
breeze

Power

Argus is now building a
second
ship. this golden one's
a
solar powered, noiseless,

plane
where barring any mistaken
identity
I will be infallible :flowing
brine

flow's changeable energy,
bolidic
residue, in 1. eight giga- pixel's
falling
block of wood from beloved

ship
onto my unassuming head-
death
from 20,000 miles away
fleeced forever

No need

to welcome this February
scam-
unwilling to resend
lies:

white fangs of winter
yellow.

I have scattered
around

flesh that now whitens
bones
into the hunger moon's
shadows.

more light than we are
used

to while usefulness
wanes

nowhere to hide, white
retracts

Post ignition

Only with a rude
laugh,
cosmic comic, is it
possible
to regulate oneself
as
mere pollution, light
pollution,
the way undistinguished
pain
works its way into a light
in
ones brain-flashing wince

would that I stopped
evolving
except in crystal. How
simple
life is without any light
playing
off the planes of shear
successive
fractures, crypts, where we
assume
an understanding how much
heat
and cooling out it was that

made us in the first: facets
of
reflecting snow beguiled
with
an unfathomable sense of
what
lies below in the compact
darkness
and what began as a laugh
turns
vague, then pixels to
apprehensive,
solstice to solstice

With

this much snow falling,
piling
on the horses, they stand
still
by the occluded fence
waiting
for it to disappear
altogether
in the bright, encompassing
light
heavy snow always brings
here
And the anticipated song's
simple
lyrics, words bouncing
between
tranquilizing flakes:
Horse!
Sally! Max! breaks
through
our reverie knowing barn
door's
open we hone in with
uncertain
feet catching on commas
hidden
in the depths of white
towards
sedulous barn door
heat

Well

Would you take it
now
that I am Viking
again?
I am confused
though
migrating through
mighty
clouds, their dual
winds
rouletting my sun-
stone's
dots to nearly where
you
should be. When
weather
clears on our
long
journey back to
another
taxing spring- where
all
our rises should begin
again:
promise me no more
ambushes
conceiving those birds
back
to my sturdy shoulders

"I am not sure that I exist, actually. I am all the writers that I have read, all the people that I have met, all the women that I have loved; all the cities that I have visited, all my ancestors." JLB

How to dress for an intrusion

While it is usually better
to be alone
lying on my fenced in
trim lawn
Night pushes thick clouds
away allowing
star shine's crawl up
the link fence
over onto darkening lawn
illuminating
one unsuited leg, then the other
with weightless,
gentle tickle that my dogs used
every morning
bringing me back to life for
an improbable
feeding frenzy, without any
social wars,
mimicking spring-time Bumble-
Bees, loopy
with plenty of dandelions held
out in sun's
slide shower of heat waves,
wavering also
in our staring eyes as our
suspicion's grow
the stars suddenly hesitate in
joining me

Alone

as usual
by the falls
in spring

as usual
walking mirror
to mirror

to the applause
of water,
cut banks,

stone
striking stone
better

than I
ever played
piano

this moss
may well
have heard

it all before
might share
echoes

when one
cares enough
to listen

Underwater

I can not
believe
our motions
slowed
and we sank
in this
frivolous water

we both can
tell
the sea's still
angered
though quieter,
tidal,
down here

our thoughts,
projected
vapor, frequent
frequencies
of threes, float
quickly
through cold zones,

laze through warm
ones
bursting on surface
contact
alerting everyone
that
we are here, here

Light

The light
this morning
opens
on tracks
that circle
the house

thankfully
a noose
made by
one,
whatever
it was,

that ringed,
round and round
attempting
to see
my sore
sleep

or keep
me here
in bouyant
ease
before the jab
of daylight

Bare handed

Leaping way out of the
gym
for the very last time
certain
to never land in any
adulation
again I stand, chest
deep
in incoming tide, watching,
waiting
the new school I am
bound
to chase; praying to
great
grandfather's grandfather
who
did the same when the
land
grew too hot, driven
to such
cool with slippery fish.
This
will no longer be
about
triple-threats, step
backs,
crossovers- what were
they
all about anyway-
no
this will be done anaerobically,
slow
rewards, with copied gathering
nets
and certainly no time-outs.

Pages

While the pages
last
paper monuments
grow
and if that Neap
Tide
of our old age
means
I have to muddle
around
somewhere in the
middle
leaving the full
flood
to our children with
its
companion low, low
tide
then I might as
well
start digging around
that
wonderful space
for
surf clams to cut
up
for our chowder

Stirrer

you're usually more
astute:
it seemed so gradual,
paint
stirrer swirling us , over
all
these years, that I have
never
attempted to tell you
how
above all else I simply
fear
my mind's playing with
carpet-
forms that light then flit,
change
because I've not invested
enough
of myself cinematically,
vocally
into real friendship, dream-
like,
or even attempted to
share,
draw a weightless,
first
proof for our fridge
door.

Tasting

Our only way out
is in
love with a medium

whose dory hopping,
planet
to planet, sees all

our world's not all!
If
we could spell

amino oarsmen
casting
gingerbread ripples

drying in dazzling
sugar
clothing we speak

of not knowing
what
is behind the clouds

or who is drawing
shapes
we are assuming

Markawasi

large stones should not
move
when viewing no matter
the time
of day or comfort of the
seat

the stones that affect
you
most bear light's
effect
on shadows that keep
us

guessing while singing
crystals
averted eyes still burn
from
this newer darkness.
What's

gone from my frame of
reference,
self, is not an imagined
animal's
willing suspension of
belief

that I am of a different
world
carved with less solid
rock
as to render subtle
move-

moment before I too
leave,
without direction, and
someone
else pays to walk this
trail

Rain

This is a good
April
drizzle on softening
soil

come stand in the
cold
and subdued, dank
hues

sodden, soaking
into
the hidden water
table

I am out feeding
birds
even though none
fly

not in imagination
or
trees where they huddle
unseen

observing while I stand
on
spongy earth as though
I

Old Burn, New Burn

too will be nourished
so
other birds can fly
having

been fed elsewhere,
leaving
trees unknown to naked
eye

existing in warm-footed
sun's
quavering air while I
doze

Still

an empty fireplace even-
though
I had gathered all that
hook
or crook, arguing, had
hurled
against our fragile house

now wicked at the floor
of
happiness tampers my,
any,
squirreling and unsure the
under-
story would condone me

till I lifted a heavy branch
from
the Norway Pine seedling
bent
as strong winds had pruned
a large
maple branch during the night

still as we both straitened
bent
backs looking for sunlight,
carbon,
that flowed through us
from
deeper mycelium roots

lent from a smiling canopy

Today

what's left of lake-ice
seems
polished by damn
damp
evening winds

when you've become
older
traveling in storms-
older
territory becomes new

again while your land-
marks
disappear in egg white
secrecy
of rime ice that's come

ashore, sublime whine
and
roar against car door,
wolf
fangs rattle, gnash the

heated windshield
while
arthritic hands twitch the
steer-
ing wheel of a car long

sold to that dull, dissatisfied
relative,
nephew, proud to be called
Buck-
wheat. Buck Wheat

Maybe

It was spring-cold
with
damp wind blowing
through
us on that hillside

I remembered how
much
I wanted to put some-
thing
living from me in that

casket. How much I
intended
to introduce father to the
crickets,
worms, bacteria that

surely would dissolve
him
in their intervening time
without
really knowing him. I

should have shoveled
in
hearse-exhaust, jumped
in
with his casket yelling,

hello, hello, anybody
home
here? This is my, our
father
please be kind, with me

Tired

I rest on the sunken
stubble
of my embattled
sofa

watching repeated
news
over and over until
one

photo garnered from
all
business security
cameras

Never a quicker
flash
hello, goodbye of
Eastern

meeting Western:
one
will sleep well
nights

while another is
destined
to stop sleeping,
loving

his spot in parental
desires,
dreams of his well
being

My, my

The loosening soil of
spring
flows over me so
operatically

sliding on a wooden
stage
brightening warm
sun-

shine replaces moon
mimicking
stars lengthy shelf life
hung

so long. So long to clear
cold
nights of soft wailing
trumpets

stiffened arms give
way,
I would love to gravel-
bloom,

blossom color through
your
softening yard, your soft-
tening

Old Burn, New Burn

stare while your stiff
attempt
to follow such
fast

color lightens you,
frightens
you as you, we, play
on

Sutter Buttes

holy, that looks a lot
like
my heart sitting out
there
on the fence, or the
world's
shortest mountain,

it has done it again
crept
out onto the porch
railing
left ventricle gasping
while
the redpolls who

themselves await their
turn
at the full feeder with
the patience
atrium, pulmonary
artery
and aorta ponder

where will I fly first this
spring
and what am I seeking
in such
a wind that blows every
thing
onto this shortest mountain

Old Burn, New Burn

that climbing up remains
a hill
but coming down equates
a mountain
of Garthic proportions
never
the less a climb for me

Fossil like

they had slowly risen
from
the floor of a missing
sea

where they had settled
when
their oxygen utilization
ended

Now their coffin uptilted
so
long ago that it seemed
they

could wriggle free by
weather's
ability to split prized prison
slabs

of slate and their souls
seem
stern as you glaze, glue
them

to the sub-floor of a
monstrous
log cabin. Unable to move
for

a second life time, word-
less,
resolved to see above haloed
reflection

Sunday Drive

Lighter than Saharan
sand
morning fog feels
its
way through the copious
obituary
of newly burned fields'
char

In lieu of flowers
for
last years wave of
harvest
blue, the old burn's
hell
sends pale stalks on
through

While Iceland

the island splits
apart

there is no tedium,
despair

bones in drekkingarthylur
rattle,

swirl in the graveyard for
lusty

women, confused, fearful
of

an index of suspicion, of
crusts

going seriously: a particular
malady

being considered during
diagnosis

We have never seen
an object

like this so early in
the universe,

our universe, where all
dark

matter's versifying
lighter

Old Burn, New Burn

light's energy, bending
space-

time looking for any
weak

points, parting the cloudy
sea

for escaping Moses
while

we chase around any-
thing

that moves robin to
song

imagined on Vioey
island

Then

out of the sunlight:
tall
and Phallic, erect,
whining
in anticipation and
debris
the pencil storm
moves
across the earth,
probing
for those who will
always
stop to see- not to
become
pillars of salt but
refuse;
yet worst of all is
for
those huddled in
dark
buildings built to
keep
wolves at bay, out,
doors
fling while unseen
silken
dust settles, wolves
growl

No response

but windblown and very
wet
still with all this flush
I

have grown to watchful
petal
crouching near to my taste,
with

the dullness of teen, where
we
are staging agents who love
to

twitter our color to all
half
mad, asthmatic tinker's
frenzied

feet tickling us down in
disarray
before flying off and barely
giving

time to primp ourselves
as prime
for the next thud of mad-
ness

My dream

Always
in a darkness where
shapes
are not permanent,
unreal,
and desperate cards
of sleep
shuffled through the
quiet
night are so out of
place,
driven here to continue
returning
to hands, will begin again,
over,
before the forming sun
insures
survival I can affirm,
torment

My apologies

but
these words have all died,
easy,
they're helpless under warping
covers

and I tell them, again, how
sorry
I am, really, to have done
that
to them all but I could

not
help myself helping myself
when
they were alive and well and I
randomly

snatched them, mid-air, bathed
them
and with military precision,
placed
them on, in, restrictive lines

listening
to their merry making until
they
realized what I had wrought,
done,

and how now they wont be
released
until an intercom hopefully
picks
them up and starts to read

Glaciers

have always disappeared
somewhere in transit

oh and then their mountains
too seemed so alive then not

this is my favorite thesaurus
an early morning crackle,

hiss to pave the outwash, onto
a moraine that looks back up

as a pure blue silence is dethroned,
nothing likes being compared

its innocence simply jettisoned,
and what would be verifiable

today if people suddenly resisted,
refused to allow you to fail

became discontented with your
crashing vulnerability,

weary beyond silent borders
and the echoing calf's call bringing

Old Burn, New Burn

past news out of fissures, feebly sliding
slow into erratic past and fanning

this perfect weave that will fill
terminally, before stepping lightly

up again to another glistening braid,
bearing dangerous calves as the

first light of sun peers down
unaware of the loosening gravel

Why

never was best at
reporter,
vast unconquered
dreams
fearful, slow steps

What was that
scratching
noise on the ground
below
my falling head

Who laid this one
golden
egg of I on the Atum's
fertile
starry ground

Where will all this
baby
turtleing bring us to
but
slowing and stowing

pixels of a life that
Queen
Earth had given a
moment
ago from warm sands

Old Burn, New Burn

Or was it Leda, rump
still
quivering heavenward
procured
a shell for my immanence

How did this sun
know
what it takes or
why
dusty dusk will always

Mira

miraculously this is
it
no more pressuring
the blind
alley of adaptation-
ah
the last generation-
sorrowfully
the women in my
family
have long ago
abandoned
severing the umbilical
cord
with their teeth and
have
left the placenta's
scent,
essential re-vitamins,
for
ravens or raccoons
who
hop around excitedly
circling
for gorgeous certainty

Worse
my doctor tells me
my
gaiety of articulation
wends
back to dactyls of
fear
or now without cartilage
slows
my steps while I
complain
our silence in the mere
death
of our long lineage

Man

Hell man this is
about
the silence one
gets
standing in family
plots

you can't pack
us
all in a can
of
headless, small
fish
some in water, oil
for
your different tastes

we just got too
old
sitting on the wharf
watching
sunrise, sunsets
while
beautiful Helen sailed
away-
the nail must be
presented
to the hammer-

Old Burn, New Burn

and by now even a
second
cup of coffee
fails
to sharpen vision
once
so clear inside our
minds
that we could
argue
hopefully she's
not
coming back no matter
what

Dang

Alas, I have properly petered
    out in Mystic.

Wish
to reconstitute myself in
    a glass of

water
while chewing on a leaf, an,
    orange maple

leaf.
Alas, I have spoon-drowned
    myself again

while
my whole state of Connecticut,
    sticky,

swoons
in air-conditioned, damp heat
    Alas

Up on Brasstown Bald

I was castling in this air,
remembering
icicles that hung,
drifted
down from the eaves
past
my bedroom window
while
my breath steams in
almost
triple digit heat and
even
my shadow has
warmed
considerably as I
attempt
to make amends for
such
a long, inadvertent
period
of non-pairing, where
many
neighbors sense my
pall
as they attempt igniting
July
fireworks between cloud
bursts
and then my own waning
I:E:D's
in this night's sapient
errand,
huddled in the law of
attraction

You

Aspiration
expiration
free slippage

you may have
won
your trip of a life-
time

somewhere more
exotic
than under mosquito
netting

it is never the now
we
pant as it closes
in

on us, on my tenuous
foot-
hold in the red hammock
churning

Free Range

Chickens
for a full week
now,
maybe more, a shadow
passed
over open octagonal
stop
signs that kept raptors,
raccoons
out and yet this shadow
now
also glides the ground with
ebbing
tides wet patience.
Stones, grass roots, beetles

pause
in their plight for water
but
the domestic chickens do
not
seem to mind: locked on
they
have done their work,
grass,
bugs romp in gizzards
and
roosting torpor allows no
fear
observing the damp
gliding

Anhydrous

I have returned, hot, sultry,
branded
a wholesome Puritan,
on
an, *our*, anniversary,
different,
heavier with salt
for
the last happy days of
blister
before tale tailing off
to
parental observation
of
Hell unable to recognize
same
or any lure that slowed
my
path in easeful rapids
tearing
out of a eager lip,
hungry,
always falling ocean-
ward
where all the sharks
called
me out of the estuary
into
multifarious deep
promise

Still have

difficulty coaxing the
inert
sense of my November
self

makes me wonder
why

I had stopped in
the first place
to watch you walk
away

in my favorite floral
dress

wait, wait I wanted
to shout
till you turned , came
back

to my, our, agony. I
felt an imaginary cheek
tear

while I stood a static,
indulgent heart simply
pumping waking me
systemically

and still I waited, waited
knowing you're eight hundred
miles and unable to walk the
hand

in hand out in our imaginary
sea

Lost America of Love
Alan Ginsberg

Dreams of becoming
lie
heaviest in the cold
desert
or fallow sidewalks,
barred
store fronts, greasy
glass
and still they come
across
hostile borders holding
hands
while stumbling in night's
pitch,

heading
past helmeted, grim-faced
survivors
of Elis Island: uninterested,
unwilling
to hear your story of
exodus,
fried food. Abundance
they've
heard it all before: oh
yeah
right here on the corner
J.D.
Rockefeller threw out
dimes
for hungry children to
scavenge

Who looks inside awakens
Carl Jung

Cool mists this
morning

I make my way
onto
ledges of Pongour

Falls with care
not
to dislodge algae

Now unable to see
past
the falls nor can

I recognize forms
of
indehiscent monks

preceding me but
am
aware they sense

my algal disruption
while
they ignore my plight

in the cool mists
this
morning

Russell Buker

I'm 74

you would think
that
after all these
years
I would have
gotten
it right: passed
through
the egg-shell door with
porcelain
knobs with a simple
twist
of the wrist and
entered
the well dusted room
where
you always sit in my
mind.

you look up, tenuous,
as
usual nor is there ever a
chair
next to you so I
sit
on the arm of your
chair,
hold your hand and look
into
your eyes but then, always,
the
other you come into
my
room wondering what
to
cook for supper and
wont
let me grab her hand.

one's
enough what's for supper

Baguette

I heard my *Hello* Raven
calling
this morning, he's
practicing

on a neighbor's scare-
crow
but we've been talking
like
that for years now

except he no longer
pauses
after my rendition
Raven-

ish speech so he
flies
nearer knowing his
nest

and all within are safe
while
we exchange our
pleasantries

we do not rehash the
drama
of made up news
bites

Old Burn, New Burn

for she knows that
when
the hunger season,
Bastille,

hits her young that
I
will arrive every morning
with

bread, no matter the
weather
or how many times
Liberty
Bells strike here and
abroad

Secrets and Sense

How much secret.
How much sense
was left
the day we put our
father down:
down through all that
had been us before
while four
of us watched his
casket bump, scratch
through the rough
spots we already knew
before and now watched
again, doctor-
like, when veins begin
to fill with too much
residue,
where tabla rasa allows
the kiss of renewal
plagiarized
with old secrets,
with new sense

Sir

I see that I have more
or less
caught your ear in
this
time of waning batteries
and
can tell you that I never
allow
myself any prolonged
rest

however imponderable
it
may seem by my reiterating,
ging,
birdlike song of the new,
smooth
nest built much later,
gilded
by myself, with a new
name

what would you bring
back
afraid and throwing twigs,
things
at the hidden radar
guns-
but as no one came to say
good-
by I built my newest me
solo

Equals

squirrels are squabbling
beyond
my porch: they are
robbing
or being robbed in the
curious
way mother takes back
balance
on an ever teetering
scale
where the weighty silence
surrounds
the sharp, insistent noise

forcing
my parents to remain
in
those lighted cemetery
chambers
knowing not a thing about
sun-
light gripping the grass
around
their headstones or that the
quiet
surrounding those inert stones
equals
enough to maintain their
silence
underneath no matter
what
I have done, now, to
provoke
mother's pointing finger

river

the river Lethe is so
damn
deep in the middle

honey
don't worry about
it

in endless brave of
self
we have spent all

being
orderly and now it
seems

not to matter: tired
dogs
always just bark

worried
in their inabilities
not

gone more like
around
the bend for a

while, gone out
of
experience somewhere

Those

those of us that
would picked
up

the single sounds
their home town
sang

your father was
a very difficult
man

beginning rain on
layered dust
grown

thicker every year-
is a difficult
man-

watching round balls
of morning dew
roll

confidently down
steep stems of
life's

slow hurtle that
most silent towns
are

Old Burn, New Burn

adamant for before
savage rains drive
us

under the cover
that dripping leaves
afford

Thankfully

trees are unable to
speak
so that we can
hear-
that is the wind
playing
bark and leaf
songs

once lived in a house
where
wind stuttered
before
finding corners to
slip
around- whistle
by

never knew if I
was
supposed to sit,
heel
or follow till it
tired
of me and my being
me

What can you bring
back
when someone has
taken
while the helter goes
on
in my life but those
sturdy

trees maxed out
slowly,
always do the sensible
thing
even if a branch was
broken
by winter storm-
weight

certainly tiny roots
twine
with similar species
slowly
savoring action above
while
sharing nitrogenous
dessert

Flash

I've redoubled
my
efforts to no avail
and

here we are you
and I

I can see you
reading
though you are
unable

to see me but I
can

shine on you-
flashlight-
and rub the angles
of
your thoughts
between my fingers

for hope
till my reflection goes
out

Old Burn, New Burn

you will have to
dig in
an underground vault
to see
such light again

as you settled out
at
a cooler temperature
much
cooler but first

Alacrity

Seems that the only
morning note for me
stems from my cat

my poor cat's timid
steps is all: she's
hyped up, hopped

up playing in soil
by the door while
friends drop their

chins as I, wedding
guest supreme, attempt
not to beleaguer

still with such a
crabbed fuse grown
down into a stunted

muse who lately
keeps silent to her-
self more and more

my personal pronoun
lips soured milk's
cold refractions

Personal pronoun

the volcano erupted-
watched from elsewhere,
another star to my TV

I wondered how often
the quintessential
diamond that is me

had gone through this
reduction/eruption
phase or if I, the me,

was always one of us:
diamonds of tissue,
bones and wishes,

and insight burning,
coming back and re-
claimed for the altar

of light within these
three energy systems:
holy oxygen utilization

oozing from the plentiful
sea in bite-sized drips
on channel fifteen news

Wall

when I'm wall-
flowered
temptation is to
dance
with Greco-Roman
legends

Like the Bay-Watch
babe
who launched 1000
ships
into the oily-blue
Aegean

her older husband
kept
her for ceremonies
and so
this strange younger
dude

sailed on an erection
all
the way home, whee
whee,
to another country
greeted

by his greatly pee-o'd
bro
who gave him what for
for
putting everyone on
Jeopardy,

categories they knew
nothing
about and couldn't
respond
quick enough with signaling
devices

night

in a dark night
one
must have an ear
listening
to trees
and
sugary sap flowing
from a tongue
talking
to trees
when the sun
comes up
it is too
late

White poof

from now on there
is no recovery.
dried

leaves drop early,
crackling, shipping out
solo

the goldenrod, tansy
ragwort, evening
primrose

saw thistles warp
into golden meadows.
milkweed's

white poof floating,
waving as black-
eyed Susan's

nod and fireweed have
climbed their peaks-
calendar-

while I, tame scare-
crow, brought to,
await winter

SH (1939- 2013)

Well that's that
and what of it

will it still now
that he's gone

will there ever
be another, some

one pissin the rest
of us off-

so balanced, so
smooth you'd

think someone else
was doing it

while he stood with
his jaw going, going-

farewell but not good-
by for the next one

who pops up
will stand on your

shoulders and be up
to him not to fall

Lies my lake told

One coming night
three wood ducks

vertical from water
softly lying to them,

please I won't stiffen,
and fly past solid

stone grey ledges,
weighted down

by star-light to a
mere mile-astonish-

ments I have posted are
beyond those shadows,

behind the slowest
shine they see, and

where magnetic lines
wool-woven with algae,

too cold to eat,
hustle wing beat

down a strange day-
light of silence

pregnant with green
slime and its sound

2 voices

every
night I lie on
a
sway-backed, rusty
cot,
cover myself in
two
sheets of sugar-
nothing
gets out but what's
necessary
to talk to everyone

how I love to sway in
minds
wind compensating
closed
doors and windows
on
the sultriest nights,
stall less,
while flighty flesh
floats
teasing worms under
this house

She was

gone well
before she disappeared

wise owl
tantalizing mirrors

only spoke
to her hated image

through limpid
eyes habitual reflection

as though
mere mirror could

draw souls
owl-eyed, with haunting

cries from
a diminishing body

that did
footprints or great

paragraphs
of fertile dust

Spontaneous
Gambol

Foreward

No matter what it is you have named me it is getting colder and colder in my house and I tire of putting on more clothing. Walt Whitman arguably said it best: Know your work and the need goes on and shall go on but, of course, it was never, for me, about becoming rich or famous rather building a sustainable life for myself as a writer which continues for me in spite of there being little left of the world I knew, what little remains is clear and the scent pervades and there should come again times when I need to remember those feelings accompanied by a relief of using it. I feel, firmly held, that poetry is still going strong all the time: in an underground stream in its Karst topography, wind free in the trees or as a celestial hum in our universe .because as Celan noted, we poets sleep in language making toward something where regular words/syntax soon become inadequate. Soon, too soon we are lost nor can we say what it was that lead us here to this, as Robert Duncan so aptly hypothesized, one becomes a disturbance of words, that have lain dormant, worse, helpless until I could begin to feel their heat tremble throughout my bones becoming clearer and clearer, the scent hovering the way those trees I had selected remembered the nick of my chainsaw

Russell Buker

Contents

it

always happens
after the dock
has

been brought in for
the coming winter
that

the weather imitates
the best we've had,
summer,

just sit on the deck
wishing cool waters
washing

so it must be, imagining,
early on after dying
would

we wish to come back
for one more opening
door

allowing the dog to
roam his nosey route
while

cool, fall grey clouds
thicken to black across
the lake

leaning this way, oh
yes, coming this way
again

always

always
the paradoxical road
lightly

traveled. always a
ringing
in ears between the

anticipation
after turning the car's
key:

words gather swiftly
choose
to depict for me

an
image with lonely rabbit
wire

hidden
in underbrush I've
been

drawn to since youth
with the
trapping hope of

something
to hold up in sunlight
unaware

that this is another scent-
song,
all I'll ever hear

Moses

who will
bury
the constant rain
sliding
winter frost's work
down
the mountain
side.
We were
warned
about living
with
our toes in
water-
hang on Moses
we're
coming in early
morning's
liquid wind, desert
mirages
sister, that images our
lake
emptying and trout
schooling
in deeper water
moving
room to room
bloated
with old odes
fallen
in the guise of
fall
May-fly hatch

Russell Buker

Lament for 75

you can not look at
yourself
in my poems now

my hands
have grown rosy, softer,
are empty

and some mornings can
not feel
bright sunlight resting

on them
thank goodness sight
has not

left me also as I
tell them
how this

years autumnal angle
of incidence
seems warmer than any

I remember-
remember not in degrees
of heat

or rutting as I pushed
your chair
faster than wheels dared

4

to go
down that gravel road
when we

lived by that talented lake
and I,
we, had reasons for taking

on the day's slow trickling
where we
knew where we were

supposed
to be and since when,
yes when

In direct

silence today is violating
my ears:
when childlike in

winter we
would all sit on snow
under electric

and telephone wires and
pretend to listen
to swimming, quick voices

It is not
good to sit under those
dark wires

mother said at breakfast
but it
has all changed now:

more wires, taller
poles, fix
my own breakfast-

all visuals,
garbled text, chaffing
snow

Assurance

it is as
though
we have enough
insurance

for the yellow
of Birch, Poplar
apostled to give
us our fall

all the foliage
we think
we deserve
before the bare-

ness of the
trees that looks
as though
everything has

fallen
through ice
for surely the
last time

oh those buoyant
baubles:
my breath, my
father's too

Beethoven's
and yes by god
Alexander
the Great's

The vase

sits with its
crystalline
memories:

15 two
15 four
and a pair

is six
in unison
mulligans too

my feet
flowering
liquids

silently,
singing,
chasing

numb
turgidity
what should,

what can
one do
footless

remembering
marathon's
sad end

on the steps,
seeds plopping
in still water

etched
by sun
in the glass

Lately

it seems
many of us are
leaving

trees
of spring and summer's
trap

we
were watching our
bios

tell
me just where
you

want
us to go this
time

among
the last colors
floating

on
the lake's surface
while

only
the nape of my
neck

remains
cold to your rough
touch

as
we have left our
accom-

plish-
ments in so many
still

houses,
with friendly windows
staring

Alien

No one dares breathe
straight
ahead, no one wants
to die
damp and so alien

My eyes feel wet,
watery
in the blue-black
late
in the mobile of night

I stand in knee-deep
river
mud where eels burrow
under
my supple soles

Far away the flash
arcs
quickly and whoever
it was
has joined the stars

that will shine on the
river
bottom tomorrow
among
dark, unconcerned eels

All

my will, my name
and
the birds have left-
recordings
vary- worse my love
died

there is no need
at all
to keep sending
catalogues

unless, of course,
you've
a new delivery
system

and are willing to
accept
changed currency,
trans-

lucent blueberry
light,
serenities' vagueness
along

with re-establishing
her
needs long forgotten
hi-

beams she never
dimmed
for the oncoming
traffic

Now

his song
was that
of an old
bull pine

how first
he breathed
at the expense
of others

how the field
in front was
cleared, burned
everyone yelling

how the trees
returned in shade
and comfort
excitedly talking

underground
recording their
own histories
How the wind

at its meanest
had stripped every
one of branches
while Hunter's

Moon circled
sunset to dawn
urging to take,
take it slow

and winter snow
will ignite
a new leaders
rising flow

shadows

I stand on a
wide lawn
flopped
to the lake

wondering
where every-
one
is today

there are
no hands
in
the landscape

of the next lake
over:
could be
the shadow

has drawn
it away
or
we have not

arrived there
yet, but
I hear
what seems

to my dulled
ears a baby
crow
hmm it is

mid October
so perhaps
it is
starving-I

would not
want such
a
short sentence

unless I
was the
only
one here

With

fantasy running on
empty

should be begging
for

anther day at least-
wasted

too many so far-
with

the spread of music
and

filing the rasp
of

cold thought down
final

will and testament
over

my toast mornings,
waiting

for daylight to begin
picking

up branches stormed
from

elderly Cedars in the
dark

key of C. Thanks to
every-

one for the bread,
toast,

body to bend again,
again

belief

is more hot butter
sliding

around the skillet
of

my dreams. in grief
I've

torn words apart to
fit

onto your page-Bede
said

that we are all Anglo
English-

seeing might be
believing

believing might be
seeing

as I tear pieces
from

my brain to paste
geo-

metrically on a page of
thirsty

light and I soon am
walking

on all fours calmly to
im-

print your long, dark
fingers

for all to see delicious
nakedness

Windmonath

Grandfather never knew
how close
he was to being right:
always
keep heading into wind's
foam-spray,
lovely option. I adore
having such
an option. I now know
the divide
between us and pounding
sea rain
is so great that I can
choose not
to listen to the slow
slump of osteo-
poritic bones caving under
his veil of taut
skin's flickering luminary
or that my
options have been taken
for granted
in the scowl of his weather:
frantic
at being caught afloat,
independent,
partly in the might of
his right

And foremost

this first snow
begins to cover
summer's gold
already diminished

count ourselves
among this diminution
although we have
been saving a little

of ourselves all along,
a savings account,
to spend on god knows
what in the unknown

future that we do not
know enough about, an
upcoming vacation that
we may or may not get,

perhaps saving any built
up residues to cash in
when we are no longer
here wandering thought-

less with flashes of our
selves calling attention
the way shooting stars
do when the sun sets

I always swim

in my matinee after
noon. How much of me
will sweep

to the same sandbar that
I caught myself up on
yesterday

how much of me today
will be the same old,
same old

or will the same
amount fetch up in the
same place

Oh, and what of the
rest that slipped,
hooray,

downstream into faster
water over-confident
by now

and lost to any radar
screen that we are
aware of

Flight

Neither Homer, or his
mother,
Naukrate, dared tell
that
Ikaros had a soft belly,

deep
desire to distance him-
self
from the compact
mind
of his father who
started
him off on his flight
too early

and thereby missed the
cooler
flight a setting sun would've
allowed,
flying over the horizon's
rim
into the densest airs of
scary,
darkened night, or, if

Hercules
would have been able
to track
where his body finally
lay

mm

My goodness! I'm here
only remember
morning dishes, turning
the sponge
along the edge of the sink

transformed blue sponge
turned left
onto the bubbles of long
highway
as I have all this month

on remote, cruise control
simple task
when there does not seem
to be
any oncoming traffic

the car has parked itself
neatly
between yellow lines in
acrid
exhaust of parking garage

I walk into your whiteness
still driving
and you partly awake also
we've had
no breakfast, heartbeats

till now and you say that
we've had
fifteen good years- don't
leave me
here- drive me home

Sore

from rebuilding someone-
elses house around the bend
where

I am tragically adept at being
ignored, steered clear of,
Haredin,

with the ultimate verses
going, gone mainstream
fearful

and trembling I approach
salvation- Jesus I am so
isolated

in my shameful sincerity,
grown used to trial and
error,

hold nothing dearest, sit
with Blake for breakfast
naked

and waiting, waiting the
loan of passion in gathering
clouds

Van

I stand before you burping
their bland
words, today's deceptive images:
if the plan
is to forgive them: let's just
say that those
machete hacked women
and children
were silent straw targets for war

how I love to renew,
myopically,
so close to your painting,
allow myself
to see violence, anger in
colliding hues
radiate, flow over me so
that I should
step back while still
attacked as
circumferential wheat straw

No need Vince as I'm
already captive
my rent in areas, whatever
else held
dear is floating in the tides
of cobbled
streets And the museum guard
loves me,
quietly holding my hand
step back
dear you are doing it again
please step

Don't

kiss me I'm dirty-
I
die everyday my
self.
this life is a real
fantasy:

holiday leftovers
emulsified,
hardening in corners
of used
brain synapses that
flap

anticipatory welcomes
to the
remaining crackle of
gnaw
on the bone of my
future,

creases of lips filled
with
warming warm spreading
grease,
incessant teeth voweling
calamity

Live Trap

no, no I'm not your parent,
not
even related, call me willing
trans-
portation who also has
moved
so many times to readily
under-
stand your plump impulse's
crash
against these squared walls in
spite
of my slow, low, labored
voice
and now more uncertainty
while
now I hastily cover your- for
the moment
cage so we both can travel
star
less routes, unknown
void's
fluctuations of cortex
rationality,
car stoppage, GPS some-
where,
looking over my shoulder
so
I can at least turn you free
Bye

Yea though

Something came in the night
robbed me of all excuses
to bury the chickadee
that attempted to use my
window for an escape route

And who could blame this
poor bird? How many times
I, myself a flightless warrior,
wanted to fly from perceived
dangers with the richness of

of sun-oil clamped in jaw
Something came in the night
cushy moss for my carpet
but no digging, filling in
in this frozen, stiff soil

All I could dream about
was not being alive anymore,
walking through the sperm-
worm's moving tunnel
that came in the night

Disremember

please tell me dear,
love,

how else does
one

remember December's
sleeplessness

when itching Cedar
branches

held in mother's
wrinkled-

bone hands furrows
my forehead

or was it brow wrink-
ling wind's

attempt to curry favor
with distrust

Come on, come on
I know

envy's your middle
name

Epigenetic

We could only
try
to be counterparts
as
before: when before
we
talked about who
it
was we thought we
were
as children sprawling
into
our long bed of
sleep
with the logged on:
today
was a long day's
sun

and there it it was,
newness
utilized at first by
chance
hidden coverings
amassed
clear the wonder
as
what sleight can we
carve
or better yet what
to do
with this childish
me
disappearing in my
hands

Storm visits

youths I have easily
coaxed, coached
headlong into their
spirit world

now adrift I visit
through long
synaptic silent
staring

what do we miss
waiting while
snow piles up, soil
fills in

I offered to help
mother up
and her arm came
off just

reminiscent of one
armed dolls
my sisters fallowed,
closet sleeping

and locked in dreams
that did not
mean anything. She
sits in

a constant chair, Give
it too
the cat to play with
nurse, sure

she's been a good
friend and you
can find another arm
to poke again

for sleeps sake, for
your ease
in caring for me
tonight

after breakfast, no
after you
visit with me again
yesterday

singing the song that
goes on
and on while snow
piles up

except for dark, lilac
branches
where chickadees, and
finches open

their seeds from the
hanging
feeders of my bedroom
closets

Prey

will this warm rain
wash the icicles
from cowed trees

do what you want
before the birds
and St. Thomas

Becket riding a paint
horse on a plains
ghost dance at

wounded knee creek
where each person has
inside a basic decency

were found face down
like cowards in red
water and pink snow

before the storm was
broken and ice stopp-
ed power returned

and divine second Henry
found himself preying
on his thawed larder

What

is it that woke
me again

Oh tired, tired
this morning

juggled things
all night

ferris wheeled
table worst

as my children
sat there

the more food
they left

the faster spun
their hunger

light through them
until breaking

through the spin
cycle they

asked to be ex,
excused and

I did find my table
this morning

leaning against
chairs and

a pocked marked
kitchen wall

Parked

behind a vacant building
so rural, to cold for birds
to venture by

later we wonder if it is
for sale or if I could
afford it

with its defeated doors,
searching windows,
fluid plaster

would you be affordable
patient while I re-glaze
loose windows

before turning on the
necessary heat for our
untamed

cosa nostra with pink
flamingos on the unkempt
front lawn

not that anyone but us
would notice or care
at all

Apricity

pre-dawn hand
firms on citric
rind of frigid
air

over spiral glass
of elevation,
heights of land,
pooling

ephemeral streams,
record of water,
toward a lower
ground

how quiet dawn
slides down its
sharp angle of
incidence

a tilted sentence
bright thought
with but fallow
heat

Before

I knew
if I found your
bookmark

that you
would sensibly close
the book

so I
would not have
to explain

that the
woman who keeps
flogging

with her
large mamaries is
not you

or that
if the power holds
through cold

battering
weather that I will
fall asleep

shoulders
covered for a change
and if

I sleep
at all with pen in
hand to

write it
all down before the
sense, if

there is
any and I can go back
to sleep,
perhaps,
as the dough is in
the oven

if more
words arise before
the sense

Last chord
Il Silencio Maastricht

there is newness
in falling
snow, metered gravely
by wisps
of wind giving expanding
space,
me, the beginnings
of now:
pained and panned in
scribbles
and etchings the brave,
unasked,
looked forward to.
Vanish
these accumulations in
breast milk
rain before clouded
vision
robbing time beats us
on through
this sallow land of silent
footprints,
white stone once again

Gone

I have found
in my stone, aristocratic
islands

a love of the gypsy
red squirreled nonchalance
digging

in moss and when I
leave, roughly alone, in
wonder

on a long, irrational
wave, sense of posture
gone

except in the cloud of
froth-white that moves
me along

How

This hammock
still
sleeps gently

buoying up
my
last plateau

how can I tell
long
silenced mother

I now
tire quickly
of this

old muscular
imprinting,
physical dis-

comfort
of ten thousand
hours

to perfection
of a
meaningless

craft
or that my mother
died

to see relevance
stained
across my brow,

strained to hear my
friends
fuzzy mutters,

gathered all in
second
sleepless pain

XX

How we loved
that sturdy
jailer

who forgot
to lock our
doors

at night so
we could
allow

troubled air
of the day

into

and permeate
our smallish
lodgings

None thought
of leaving
while

slowly picking
through those
gleanings

of someone's
nameless day
with

slow, excited
archaeological
cries

of discovery -
every day born
again-

every so often
those earthen
clouds

dry as lowered
voices, indistinct,
made

ears intently floor
bound with nothing
but

the scratch of
sunlight under the
door

Struggle ever renewed (WW)

Shiny lady
with taut body

the nickel and dimes
we play with

bounce off
your playful

limbs, your
smile is energy

for all down-
hill hopefuls

then, oh my
god your chest

opens up again,
heart expands

the next thing
I know I'm in

your aorta, part
of your heartbreak:

white haired
corpuscle to your soul

Charles Fredrick

my dream always
wandering through mist
and early lake sun

I do not know how
alone I have become in
branches of sunlight

my parents can no
longer feel this sun and I
have a new grandson

they should have loved
you even in the monotony
of their windless mist

be still I hear you
the thickness of love transparent
left lung rooms my heart

cool blue and green foliage
moves me in tar-mac's loud pour
toward home, joy, you

Twixt

That was yesterday's
today
seems forward progress
has been
stopped, unfettered
seize
of pictures from the local
newspaper
will not move on: only
imagined,
willed communications
to
sown fields, regenerating
wood-
lot will have to make
doodley
do in spite of yesterday's
prostrate
behavior, face down, and
today's
white sheets, bagged drips
dropping
between each other before
tripping
through dull, unsuspecting
veins
pumping the days news
of crimes
to the body, nurses ad-
vertising

drawn curtains with light
that seems
so unnecessary now in
all the
channels of yesterdays
failure
to completely compute
saplings
white roots fumbling
through
the dark earth in hope
that
today will become yesterday's
tween

tu me manques

Kudos, I think, to
those
who saved us when
all was
saddened to dust

this bilious I now
reside
can often snap
out
in a mares tail

impossible to tell
you
when this happens
unless
someone downloads

my file for since
being
uploaded I have no
say
in any interpretation

and only exist at some
ones
beck back on earth,
if it
still exists at all,

nor can I tell you
of
anyone else who is
riding
this jet stream of

the internet or where
we are,
have been and our
bio's
incapable telling all

I know

it is Candlemas
we buy them now
waiting

for local shadow's
fortune tales easing
the grip

weather has had
on mother who
sits

in her pseudopodic
sensory ingestions
watching

a bowl of an old
favorite, Chrysanthemums,
floating

in ice cold water.
River, river she yells
to her-

self- another dead
branch broken off
cleanly

at the synapse by
the winds of her
memory

to be picked up
for fireplace fuel
by me:

is this all I wonder
it seems so like the
beginning

except for our family
heritage that trails
generation

to generation in a
quest to out pencil
notes

of one armed bandit's
celestial song anyway
we can

When the plane lands

and I visit
do not be alarmed

when I tell you
that soon, too soon

you will become
patriarchal, which

sounds like a
slap of responsibility

but no just
become an authority

of version,
whatever you know

of our selves:
they all took their share

out of the middle,
places been to clamoring

for attention as
you now stand in the

swell of light
that measures your time

so be gentle
with it for time's

grains of glass
beach on a distant

shore that we
know nothing about

and soon, too
soon again, we will be

wet with light,
dazzling expansion

Before the cow jumps

fish will let us come
home:
now I've bee granted
future
I suppose I should
agree
with those who think
late
night travels, alone,
aimless
with hopefully a full
slate
of stars: my gill net
spoons
trawling deep to find
out
what is farming way
out
there in the reel shoal-
ing
daylight full-filing my
skiff

Nothing

but snowstorms this
late into February

migrating robins
sing in heavy

woods, drawn north
by Sirius B

revolving around
Sirius A, better known

for our complaints
summer heat brings

but I am now
down to red squirrel

subnivium near my
bird feeders where

I have only hope
the robins will forage

for hope alone is
an awkward thing

to mouth with the
calendar holding

the shoveling, full
flakes of moon in

both our guessing
hands, guessing

Frieze

As one who often
falls asleep
in restaurant booths
over breakfast
it is slowly possible
to perceive
myself in you: we
walk in mist,
wet fog- you were
always willing
to devour but now
red, rusted
hands startle you-
a wind from
somewhere pleads
for remember,
wisps me everywhere,
desires to
remain, this much
moisture or
eyelids roar may
never come
this way ever again

Vistas

planning on moving,
again,
visiting you, amazed
to be
jostled so, dawdling
in my
dreams, by way too
many
skittish people street
walking
along when suddenly
remembered
I have had better eye
contact
with trees and stone
fences
who had had something
to say

Pied-a-terre

risen
bread dough,
glassy
footprints on
whales
way: where
they
have been,
where
they are
going-
dough, electricity
whales
journeys not concrete
nouns:
the way things
behave

the way Bertrand
Russell
looked at his
non
hand after it was
non
cut, how did I do
that
with a knife- non
knife-
blood, dumkoff

Shrove

So, this is it
Atlantic spotted
dolphins confessing
in our alders. All

these pictures
would not have
needed to know
themselves-

I have only been
able to feed a few
hungry hawks from
stored anonymity:

beautiful boxes of
lovage, coffee pots
full of spew while
someone keeps

nibbling my frozen
shoulder the way
sharks attacked my
dolphins into alders

to safely fast in
the alder's faint
green praying
beneath the snow

Voire Dire

cadences wet with
remember
down an open
shirt,
striking me in
sleep,

there are times
when
first awake I can
only
wish for antlers,
shells

covering my grateful
totems
sensitive skins for
I have
juried and engaged
an old

soul, dreaming in
lucid
dreams where words
float,
tectonic platelets,
and I

write early these
mornings
listening to our
family
Ravens plucking
rhythms,

keeping me in step
way
before other birds
mimic
poetically correct
songs

Never airborne

An appreciation of
the anonymous poet
who died this week

why this week of
all weeks do I
have to attend

no mas, sitting there
exercising bladder control
just to get dialogue right

Do you want eggs for
breakfast or will you
sit mumbling to yourself

wait, two more lines left:
forsee my own death
so well annotated before

one would think this was
marble's slow etching
yet limestone's quicker

easier on the hands, yes
no bleeding, not much, and
no eggshells in frying pan

goodbye to you, you with
the famously difficult,
never outdated name

You called

Me phobia! but I am,
was not, far from it
on the road to there

we no longer speak
of the trees silence
to me in hot sunlight

or flowers that shake
their leaves giving
off odors that brings

hornets that hum to stamen
and leave footprints
on nodding pistles

No, I tell my stately
tree, we will have
no words even though

our origin was the
gordy tidal-pool-
before I knew her

naked light would
soon put me at a
loss for words too-

ancillary, I do not
have to tell you
about the loneliness

beyond this loop of
marching trees as all
I wanted was to believe

Then

we could use our bridges
for floral decorations,
ant farms

thank heaven we do
not just walk on hazy
air-

birds themselves even-
tually touch down not
selling

themselves short, as I
have been known to,
disrespecting

the ground we are
bound to as we (I)
preposition

our lives to: to dig, to
debris and subjugate
whatever

moves freely around
us, uneaten or painted
red,

two more degrees of
heat from our breath
will change

the very air that our
alveoli have grasped
from

mouths of histories
finest breath expired
on earth

and now this will change
to a burning sensation
no matter

how much mucous is expelled
Ah yes, thank heavens we
do not

walk on air: tethered,
grounded by an invisible
hand

that holds the barbed lure's
string and who just might let
go

Dispense

I am a heavy man
slow,
burdened by my
years

today as I walked
on
fine wind-pack
snow

paired by my belief
that
two-foot thick ice
below

will be supportive,
hedging
all bets on many
good

gigs of supposition.
You
both watched, from
our

picture window, my
slow
pace while feeding
absent

birds their old bread,
walnut,
banana cookies we
did

not finish, did not
finish